Lost in Translation

15 Hebrew Words to Transform Your Christian Faith

Eitan Bar

798857242452

Contents

Introduction

While reading the Hebrew Scriptures in translation can certainly offer significant insights, there is a particular depth of understanding that can only be reached by engaging with the text in its original language. For those who can read Hebrew, this presents a remarkable opportunity to delve deeper into their spiritual heritage and enrich their understanding of the Scriptures, enhancing both personal faith and scholarly pursuits. The cultural, linguistic, poetic, and theological insights that the Hebrew language offers are invaluable tools in the process of biblical hermeneutics and interpretation.

The vocabulary in Hebrew is rather concise, comprising roughly 8,000 words. However, this perceived limitation actually highlights the beauty of Biblical Hebrew, as it means each Hebrew word carries multiple meanings, often layered in complexity. This characteristic gives the language its unique depth. Consequently, translation from Hebrew to another language presents significant challenges. Translators must select a single interpretation, which may not entirely reflect the true connotation of the words. This not only often results in losing the richness of the original word but also risks obscuring the intended meaning behind that term.

Reading the Hebrew Bible is a complex task, but even more so for those who are not fluent in the Hebrew language. Instead, they must rely on translations to access this sacred text. While translations are invaluable resources, they inevitably involve compromises and may not always capture the full meaning, nuance, and richness of the original Hebrew text. As a result, readers who are not proficient in Hebrew may miss out on certain aspects of the text that have been either mistranslated or are simply impossible to convey accurately through translation.

The Hebrew language is intrinsically tied to the culture and context in which the Bible was written. Hebrew is a Semitic language deeply rooted in the history and beliefs of the Jewish people.

Semitic languages, including Hebrew, Arabic, and Aramaic, are part of the larger Afro-Asiatic language family. These languages have distinct features that set them apart from languages like English, which belongs to the Germanic branch of the Indo-European language family. For example, Semitic languages have grammatical gender, with nouns, adjectives, pronouns, and verbs agreeing in gender. In Hebrew and Arabic, for example, there are masculine and feminine genders, while English has lost grammatical gender in nouns and adjectives and uses gender-neutral language for most cases except pronouns (he, she, they).

For example, the Tanakh (Hebrew Bible) treats the Holy Spirit almost exclusively in the feminine grammatical form, but of course, there's a significant difference between grammatical gender and biological sex. When the verse reads, "the Spirit of God was hovering over the waters" (Genesis 1:2), it refers to the feminine in grammatical terms, not gender identity. A specific word that takes on a certain grammatical gender in one language can take a different grammatical gender in another language. This has absolutely nothing to do with gender. That's the case with the Greek word for 'Spirit' (πνεῦμα), which is written in a neuter grammatical gender - genderless. While in Hebrew, the word 'spirit' almost always appears in the feminine grammatical form, it would be a linguistic (and theological) error to project grammatical gender onto gender identity. In other words, the grammatical gender used for the Holy Spirit in Hebrew is not at all critical because, unlike humans or animals, the Holy Spirit doesn't have a gender identity.

But the main difference is that Semitic languages use a root-based system in which a set of usually three (sometimes two or four) consonants forms the basis of a word. Various patterns of vowels and affixes are added to the root to create different but related meanings. A good example is the root of the word "Hebrew" (IVRIT). The root can convey ideas related to crossing, passing, or transgressing. Here are some words derived from this root with different meanings:

AVAR: This verb can mean "to cross," "to pass," or "to go through."

IVRI: This noun, derived from the same root, means "Hebrew person" and is used to describe the Hebrew people. Genesis 14:13 is used to identify Abram (Abraham) as a Hebrew: "And there came one that had escaped, and told Abram the Hebrew (HA'IVRI)." The term is thought to be connected to the idea of "crossing over" or "coming from the other side," possibly referring to Abram's journey from Mesopotamia to the land of Canaan.

MA'AVAR: This noun means "ford," "crossing," or "passage." In Genesis 32:22-23 it is used to describe a place where Jacob's family crosses the river.

AVERAH: This noun means "transgression," "sin," or "wrongdoing." When someone is "crossing a line," so to speak, they are committing an AVERAH. It is related to a moral crossing of boundaries or committing wrongdoing. The same exact word, in a different context, also means "judgment" or "wrath." (Proverbs 11:4).

These examples illustrate how Hebrew words with the same root can have different meanings but are connected by a common idea. This can be confusing for those translating the Hebrew Bible into other languages. Hebrew is a rich language with many words and phrases containing multiple layers of meaning. This complexity poses a significant challenge for translators, who must attempt to convey the subtleties of the Hebrew text into another language while remaining faithful to the original meaning, which is not always possible to do.

Another challenge in translating the Hebrew Bible is the issue of linguistic and cultural differences. Every language is embedded within a unique cultural context, and certain words and phrases in Hebrew may not have direct equivalents in other languages. For instance, Hebrew words, as we just saw, often carry multiple meanings or connotations that are difficult to convey in a single English word. Additionally, the Hebrew Bible is filled with idiomatic expressions, wordplays, and allusions that are challenging to translate without losing the intended meaning or literary effect.

An additional challenge in translating the Hebrew Bible is the historical distance between the original text and modern readers. The Hebrew Bible was written thousands of years ago, and our understanding of the language, culture, and historical context has inevitably changed over time. Scholars continue to debate and discover new information about linguistics and the ancient world, which can impact our understanding of the Bible and its translation. As a result, translations may not always reflect the most current or accurate understanding of the Hebrew text and its context, making its interpretation challenging.

Furthermore, the process of translation inherently involves interpretation. Translators must choose how to render specific words, phrases, and passages from the original Hebrew (and Greek) into another language. These choices are often guided by the translator's understanding of the text, their theological beliefs, and their cultural background. Consequently, different translations may emphasize or highlight different aspects of the text, and readers may encounter varying interpretations depending on their chosen translation.

For this example, let's look at a passage from the New Testament. In Matthew 10:29, we see two different translations that convey significantly different meanings. The ESV emphasizes God's awareness of all that happens, stating, *"And not one of them will fall to the ground apart from your Father."* At the same time, the NKJV adds the word "will" (missing from the original Greek text) and suggests that God actively causes the death of the sparrows: *"And not one of them falls to the ground apart from your Father's* ***will.****"* This subtle change in wording leads to a vastly different interpretation of the verse (if someone dies, it's because God wanted them to die, vs. God was well aware of their death), highlighting the importance of carefully considering the context and meaning of the original text when translating or interpreting the Bible.

Despite these challenges, translations of the Hebrew Bible play a crucial role in making the text accessible to a wider audience. They allow individuals who are not proficient in Hebrew to engage with the sacred text, develop their faith, and connect with the teachings and values of God. However, it is essential for readers to be aware of the limitations and potential pitfalls of translations and to approach them with a discerning eye.

Readers can benefit from comparing different translations of the Bible. By examining various translations side by side, one can gain a better understanding of the range of possible interpretations and identify the nuances that may be lost in a single translation. This comparative approach can help readers to develop a more comprehensive and informed understanding of the text, enabling them to engage more deeply with the Bible's teachings and messages. In addition, engaging with others who are knowledgeable about the Hebrew language (and no, unfortunately, taking a Hebrew class in seminary does not make one an expert) can provide valuable insights and promote a more profound understanding of the text. Such interactions can challenge and deepen one's own understanding of the Hebrew Bible.

Benefits of Reading Biblical Hebrew

The Hebrew Scriptures, also known as the Tanakh or the Old Testament, form the basis of Jewish religious thought and practice. They are considered sacred and hold a wealth of spiritual, historical, and cultural significance. For those who can read these texts in their original Hebrew language, a deeper understanding and more nuanced interpretation can be achieved. This advantage in hermeneutics (the science of interpretation) and biblical exegesis offers several benefits.

Understanding Cultural Context

One of the most significant advantages of reading the Hebrew Scriptures in Hebrew is the direct access to the cultural context of the texts. Each language is inherently connected to the culture from which it originates, carrying nuances and idiosyncrasies that cannot be fully captured through translation. Hebrew, as a Semitic language, embodies the mindset, customs, and traditions of the ancient Israelites, and understanding this can provide a deeper insight into the narratives and laws within the Hebrew Scriptures. For example, the Hebrew word "shalom," commonly translated as "peace," carries a much broader semantic range, including wholeness, completeness, prosperity, safety, and tranquility. Therefore, when Jewish scholars read about "shalom" in the Scriptures, they understand it's not just the absence of conflict but the presence of holistic well-being.

Accuracy in Interpretation

Translation, by necessity, involves some level of interpretation. Depending on the translator's choices, subtle shifts in meaning can occur, sometimes leading to significant theological differences. Reading the Scriptures in Hebrew mitigates this issue. Consider the term "HESED," often translated as "loving-kindness" or "mercy." However, HESED encompasses love, mercy, grace, kindness, loyalty, faithfulness, and covenant fidelity. When a Hebrew speaker reads HESED they are confronted with the rich multi-dimensionality of God's character that a simple English translation might not fully convey.

Better Understanding of Poetry and Wordplay

Hebrew is a highly expressive language that lends itself to poetic structures, wordplay, puns, and multiple layers of meaning. This is evident in the Psalms and wisdom literature, where understanding Hebrew allows for the appreciation of these stylistic elements. One example is found in the story of Adam and

Eve in Genesis 2:23. Adam says about Eve: "This is now bone of my bones and flesh of my flesh: she shall be called Woman (ISHSHAH) because she was taken out of Man (ISH)." This wordplay between "ISH" (man) and "ISHSHAH" (woman) carries significant weight in the original Hebrew, emphasizing their unity and mutual origins, a nuance that is often lost in translation.

Appreciating the Theological Nuances

The Hebrew language can convey deep theological concepts that are often simplified or overlooked in translation. For instance, the Hebrew name for God, "YHWH" (often translated as "LORD"), is derived from the verb "to be," suggesting God's self-existence, eternity, and faithfulness. This realization adds a new layer of understanding when Jews read the Shema in Deuteronomy 6:4: "Hear, O Israel: YHWH our God, YHWH is one." In Hebrew, this is not just an assertion of monotheism but also a proclamation of God's eternal and self-existent nature. Some misunderstanding of Hebrew words or idioms even contributed to why Jews don't believe in Jesus.[1]

In conclusion, while translations of the Hebrew Bible are essential for making the text accessible to those who do not speak Hebrew, it is important for readers to be aware of the potential limitations and challenges inherent in the translation process. By engaging with supplementary resources, learning the Hebrew language, and comparing multiple translations, readers can overcome some of these limitations and develop a richer, more nuanced understanding of the sacred text. This multifaceted approach can help individuals connect more deeply with the teachings and values of the Bible and foster a greater appreciation for the beauty, complexity, and depth of this ancient and enduring text.

* For a further discussion on the interpretation of Biblical texts, see my other book: "Read Like a Jew: 8 Rules of Basic Bible Interpretation for the Christian."

---

1. You can read more about it in my 2023 book: "Why Don't Jews Believe in Jesus."

PEACE
Hebrew: SHALOM

If there is one Hebrew word that has gained global recognition, it is "SHALOM." Often translated as "peace," SHALOM represents an array of nuances that are far more profound and multifaceted. However, translating SHALOM merely as peace does not fully encapsulate its depth. The concept of SHALOM brings us to realize the perfection in our holy God, reinforcing the profound significance of this word in understanding the character of our Creator.

In the Hebrew language, SHALOM signifies "wholeness," "completeness," "perfection," "payment," and more. All these meanings share a common root, the foundation of their linguistic connection. The word SHALOM, a noun, also encompasses completeness, soundness, welfare, harmony, prosperity, and tranquility. While English lacks a single term that encapsulates all these concepts, examining the various biblical occurrences of SHALOM offers insights into its more profound significance.

In Judges 6:24, for example, SHALOM is part of one of the names for God - "Jehovah Shalom" or "The Lord is peace." Having encountered God personally and witnessed His supernatural power, Gideon erected an altar and named it "Jehovah Shalom." Through this act, he proclaimed to everyone that our God embodies SHALOM - He is peace, wholeness, completeness, perfection, harmony, and prosperity in their most profound sense.

In the embodiment of Jesus, we find our SHALOM. He makes us whole. Our spiritual debt is paid in full. But this concept of SHALOM, as understood by those well-versed in

Hebrew, is not just about the cessation of conflict or the existence of a formal peace treaty. Instead, it encapsulates a state of unity, cooperation, brotherly love, goodness, and completeness, permeating every aspect of life.

The peace we yearn for must spring from our very souls, for without peace with God, we are bereft of true peace. Jesus came to reconcile this discord between humanity and God, highlighting that the absence of peace is not merely an external issue. The expectation that a warrior Messiah, as anticipated in some interpretations of rabbinic Judaism, would eradicate Israel's enemies and consequently ensure peace fails to address the heart of the matter.

One might misconstrue that peace would naturally ensue if all weaponry and means of physical violence were eliminated. However, this presumption is flawed. Animosity can manifest itself in various forms, from harsh words to systemic harassment, all of which can inflict deep emotional and psychological damage, potentially more devastating than physical harm. Removing all weapons would not prevent individuals from resorting to other means, such as stones, sticks, or even words, to inflict harm on others.

The concept of a warrior Messiah killing all the adversaries to bring about harmony is an oversimplified solution to a complex problem. Tragically, certain fundamentalist circles have appropriated this notion, prophesying Jesus's return as an army general, poised to renounce the Sermon on the Mount and vanquish billions, thus forgetting his teachings, including "Blessed are the peacemakers" (Matthew 5:9).

The belief that eliminating those who oppose your convictions will engender a utopian world is logically and theologically unsound. Christian history provides evidence of this, where millions perished in religious wars,[1] even though they shared a common faith. The present-day treatment of Christians by their fellow believers further underscores this point. A Christian friend who leads an international ministry once told me, "We, Christians, are the only army in the world that shoots its own wounded soldiers."

I firmly believe that global peace cannot be achieved through mass extermination. Instead, it is through adherence to the principles of love, humility, and sacrificial giving, as exemplified by Jesus, that true peace can be realized. His teachings encourage us to love even our enemies (Matthew 5:44), an action far removed from the call to eliminate them.

I am not advocating pacifism, and I fully acknowledge that there are circumstances where conflict may be unavoidable. Indeed, the roles of soldiers, police officers, the legal system, and prisons remain critical. However, I strongly contest the idea that the Messiah will bring SHALOM by annihilating billions. Such a notion seems inherently contradictory.

The pathway to peace that Jesus advocates commences with reconciling the rift between humanity and God. Through his sacrifice, Jesus restored this relationship, allowing us to draw nearer to God and hence find inner peace. However, Christ's death was not a means to appease an angry God but to redefine our understanding of God's nature. Unlike the wrathful gods of the pagans surrounding Israel, Jesus revealed a loving Father, ready to sacrifice all for his beloved creation. This transformation in perception can bring peace to the most embittered hearts. Once freed from hate and resentment, this internal serenity can radiate outwards, fostering peace with others, even those perceived as enemies.

In this way, the role of the Messiah in ushering SHALOM is not about eliminating opponents or enforcing a shallow peace through fear. It involves cultivating a profound peace by first bridging the gap between humanity and God. This divine reconciliation, which Jesus achieved during his earthly ministry, opens the pathway for us to reconnect with God. By following Jesus' teachings, we are also given the opportunity to contribute to the establishment of the Kingdom of Heaven on earth, a realm defined not by material riches but by righteousness, peace, and joy in the Holy Spirit (Romans 14:17).

So, when we speak of SHALOM, we are referring not just to a state of tranquility but a state of flourishing in every dimension of existence. SHALOM involves harmonious relationships with God, fellow humans, and even the natural world (Isaiah 11:6–10; Revelation 21:1–7). This broad understanding of SHALOM offers us a vision of life as it was meant to be, as ordained by God before the fall. This concept allows us to see how the peace and reconciliation brought about by Jesus are not only the end goal but are integral to every step of the journey.

In conclusion, the Hebrew concept of SHALOM, as exemplified in the teachings and life of Jesus, prompts us to think of peace not just as an absence of conflict or a state to be achieved but as a way of life that affects all aspects of our existence. In this way, peace - SHALOM - is not just something we hope for in the future but something we strive to live out in our daily lives. Therefore, let us aim to live lives characterized by SHALOM, experiencing the completeness, soundness, and tranquility that it offers.

To truly know SHALOM is to know God, for He is the "Prince of Peace" (Isaiah 9:6) and the source of all peace. As we strive to cultivate this peace in our lives and in the world around us, let us always remember that God is SHALOM - He is our peace, our wholeness, our completeness, and our perfection. By this understanding, we can start to comprehend the depth of God's love for us, His willingness to sacrifice for our well-being, and His eternal desire for us to live in SHALOM with Him and each other. This comprehension of peace, as deeply intertwined with our understanding of God, is a key to unlocking a life of profound fulfillment and divine purpose.

---

1. The wars of religion were a series of wars waged in Europe during the 16th, 17th and early 18th centuries between Catholics and Protestants.

SACRIFICE

Hebrew: QORBAN

קָרְבָּן

The word for sacrifice/offering in Hebrew is QORBAN, which comes from the word QAROB, meaning "closeness" or "ne arby."[1] So if I said that you are my QAROB, it would mean you are my relative. That Hebrew word also reflects "*to let go of something for the sake of others.*"[2]

For the ancient Israelites, the practice of QORBAN (sacrifice or offering) was fundamentally about willingly giving something valuable to establish a closer relationship with another entity. The term "QORBAN" itself stems from the root word QAROB, which denotes proximity or nearness. This linguistic connection underlines the idea that a sacrifice (whether an animal or agricultural) is not about killing something but is a deliberate act aimed at fostering closeness.

This principle is still observable in modern times. Consider organ donors, for example. The act of donating an organ is a profound physical sacrifice, and often, it engenders an emotional bond between the donor and recipient. This act of self-sacrifice, of giving a part of oneself to benefit another, brings them closer together. Similarly, when it comes to our relationship with God, drawing near to Him is fundamentally intertwined with self-sacrifice.

Under the Old Covenant, the Law required the Israelites to make physical sacrifices to God to establish and maintain this closeness. These sacrifices typically involved giving up valuable resources, such as livestock or grains, as an act of worship and reverence towards God.

However, with the advent of Jesus Christ and the establishment of the New Covenant, there occurred a significant paradigm shift in understanding and practicing sacrifice. Rather than requiring believers to make material sacrifices directly to God, Jesus taught that we approach God by making sacrifices for others. Jesus emphasized that to draw near God, one should be ready to relinquish personal possessions and help those in need:

> "If you want to be perfect, go, sell your possessions and give to the poor, and you will have treasure in heaven." (Matthew 19:21)

In other words, when we sacrifice for the benefit of others, it is considered as if we are making direct sacrifices to God:

> "Do not forget to do good and to share with others, for with such sacrifices God is pleased." (Hebrews 13:16)

So, in the New Covenant, believers honor God not by making physical offerings on an altar but through acts of kindness, generosity, and self-sacrifice for the benefit of others. Therefore, our expressions of faith should not be limited to personal spiritual practices like prayer and scripture study (though these are important too). Instead, we show our love for God and emulate Christ by extending ourselves for the well-being of others.

When we bless others, we position ourselves to receive blessings from God in return.

Think back to childhood memories, particularly to school field trips where sharing snacks among friends was a microcosm of this principle of QORBAN. In that context, snacks were valuable commodities, and sharing them was a significant act of sacrifice. It was a way to express friendship, seek favor, or make amends. This seemingly simple act of sharing reflected a broader principle of reciprocation, reinforcing the idea that a genuine sacrifice is intended to engender closeness.

These traditions of sacrifice among children echo the logic that drove the ancient Israelites' sacrificial rituals. They believed that by making sacrifices for God, they could earn His favor and secure a promising earthly and eternal destiny. They hoped to find themselves on God's "good side" on the Day of Judgment. Hence, they willingly sacrificed their wealth, time, and energy as an expression of their devotion and desire for divine favor.

Gift-giving is an everyday manifestation of the principle of QORBAN. Whether we're giving someone a modest lunch or an extravagant diamond ring, the real value of a gift lies not in its material worth but in the sacrifice it represents. More significant gifts indicate a more considerable sacrifice. Furthermore, sacrifice doesn't always have to be material - it can take the form of time, energy, privileges, pride, rights, and even body parts.

In essence, the principle of QORBAN invites us to deepen our relationships—both with God and with each other—through acts of self-sacrifice. As we extend ourselves for the well-being of others, we embody the loving, generous spirit of God and draw closer to Him. We find ourselves part of a continuum of love and sacrifice that stretches back to ancient times and continues to define our relationship with God and our fellow human beings today.

---

1. M. M. Bravmann, "Studies in Semitic Philology", P. 465-477.
2. R. J. Thompson, "Sacrifice and Offering," in New Bible Dictionary, ed. D. R. W. Wood et al., (Downers Grove: InterVarsity Press, 1996), 1035.

BLOOD
Hebrew: DAM

In this era, filled with action movies, violent video games, and incessant news reports of violence, it's hardly surprising that the term 'blood' often conjures negative associations such as violence, terrorism, war, suffering, and wrath. This perspective might explain why some preachers assert that God tortured, abused, and killed Christ. However, the Hebrew Bible approaches the concept of blood from a distinctly different angle.

In Genesis, the Hebrew words "Adam" and "DAM," meaning "blood," share a linguistic root. This commonality leads to a profound theological insight into the nature of humanity, according to the Bible. The name "Adam" is also closely tied to the Hebrew word "ADAMAH," meaning "ground." This connection is evident in Genesis 2:7, where God forms the first human, Adam, from the ADAMAH. Therefore, "Adam" signifies humanity's earthly origin. On the other hand, "DAM" (blood) represents life. (Leviticus 17:14).

DAM = Blood.
ADAMAH = Ground.

The name "Adam" intriguingly embodies a fusion of these two concepts. It can be interpreted as suggesting a deep connection between mankind (Adam) and the life force (blood) as well as the earth (ground) from which we were created. This connection suggests that while humans are formed from the earth, the blood/life force within them animates and gives them life.

Two common words can best describe the functions of blood in the Bible. If you were to ask modern-day Christians what they are, some would probably answer with something like 'wrath and punishment.' However, for the Israelites living in the days of the Hebrew Scriptures, it would probably be something like 'purifying and cleansing.'

Do you remember greeting someone with a handshake during Covid-19 and wanting to sanitize your hands instantly? Or maybe how we wash away stains using a detergent. These liquids are a great way to understand the role of blood in the biblical ritual of purification and sanctification. For the Israelites, the blood of the sacrifices was something like iodine, bleach, or detergent—a 'magical potion' used to keep and protect life.

For the ancient Israelites, blood held profound significance - it was viewed as the embodiment of life and a vehicle for purification, atonement, and healing. This concept is deeply rooted in the verse from Leviticus 17:11:

> *For the **life** of a creature is in the **blood**, and I have given it to you to make **atonement** for yourselves on the altar; it is the **blood** that makes **atonement** for one's **life**.*

The verse from Leviticus provides a foundational understanding of atonement within the biblical context. In this scripture, blood symbolizes life and plays an instrumental role in rituals aiming for reconciliation with God. This reflects the immense value placed on life in Hebrew tradition and theology. Today, we understand scientifically that our life force is indeed contained within our DNA, which is in our blood.

In Judaism, Rashi, the famous 11th-century Jewish rabbi and commentator, wrote in his Commentary on Leviticus 17:11:

> For the life of the flesh of every creature, not only of animals brought as sacrifices, is dependent on its blood, and it is for this reason that I have placed it [on the altar] to make expiation for the life of man: let life come and expiate for life!

Some things in life are inseparable. You can't make soup without liquid, build a log cabin without trees, or make a bonfire without flames. The same goes for sacrifice. Sacrifices are where life meets death—they are two sides of the same coin. Without an animal being killed, there would be no blood. The two are tied together because you cannot have the animal's blood without killing it. This is also true in our physical world—we cannot live unless something else dies, as we must eat to survive. Eating means something else—either an animal or a plant—dies. Life and death are strongly intertwined.

However, in the book of sacrifices (Leviticus), the animal substitute is not offered by Israelites hoping to appease a volatile and angry God. That is why the pagan nations around Israel would sacrifice to their gods. For Israel, it was a different story...

In the context of sacrifices, the focus was less on the death of the animal and more on its blood - the representation of life. In other words, the animal's death was a consequential necessity for obtaining its life-giving blood. Hence, the phrases 'Christ died for us' and 'Christ's blood was shed for us' can be used interchangeably when discussing Christ's atonement. Both statements aim to communicate the same profound message - Christ's death signifies the shedding of His blood.

In the sacrificial rituals, death wasn't what atoned for sins; blood did. Death was a significant, unavoidable side effect of the sacrifice. If an animal was to provide all its blood - its life force - it inevitably had to die. This death was a sort of penalty paid for extracting its blood. Thus, if someone owed their life to you, it implied they owed their blood.

In the same vein, just as the blood of sacrificed animals served to purify, sanctify, and cleanse Israel from its sins, so does Christ's blood for our transgressions. His crucifixion wasn't about him being subjected to torment and abuse by God but about His blood, symbolic of His life, washing away our sins.

This perspective leads us to the real crux of the Bible's message - it's not about the wrathful death of Christ at the hands of his Father, but the significance of Christ's blood. To state 'Christ's blood was shed for us' is equivalent to saying 'Christ gifted us His life.' This is why New Testament authors consistently reiterate that it is Christ's blood that covers our sins, redeems us, and justifies us. The true value lies not in His death but in the life-representing blood of Christ:

> *...we have redemption through his **blood**, the forgiveness of sins... (Ephesians 1:7)*

> *...to make the people holy through his own **blood**... (Hebrews 13:12)*

> *...him who loves us and has freed us from our sins by his **blood**..." (Revelation 1:5)*

> *...we have now been justified by his **blood**... (Romans 5:9)*

> *...we have redemption through his **blood**... (Ephesians 1:7)*

> *...have been brought near by the **blood** of Christ... (Ephesians 2:13)*

> *...making peace through his **blood**, shed on the cross... (Colossians 1:20)*

> *...you were redeemed...with the precious **blood** of Christ... (1st Peter 1:18-19)*

> *...the **blood** of Jesus, his Son, purifies us from all sin... (1st John 1:7)*

Because life is in the blood, it holds the power of purification, sanctification, justification, and atonement. Blood, being life, is why it was said about Jesus that unless you "drink his blood, you have no life in you" (John 6:53). It is through Jesus' life that we receive eternal life, and his life was in his blood. This means the gospel is not about death but about life! And the gospel is good news not because Jesus died at the hands of an angry God but because Jesus gave us His life! Since Christ is God, if we "drink" His blood (life), we get to enjoy everlasting life!

SIN or PURIFICATION OFFERING

Hebrew: HATA'AT

HATA'AT is a category of sacrifices that can be further divided (chicken or beef, personal or communal, internal or external, etc.) The Hebrew word HATA'AT confuses scholars because it comes from either of two words that share the same root: 'HET,' meaning "sin." Or 'HITE,' meaning to "disinfect, cleanse; purify; sterilize." In English, HATA'AT is translated both ways; therefore, you sometimes see "Sin Offering" while other times, "Purification Offering."[1] However, most Hebrew scholars and Jewish commentators[2] side with the second option, purification. They would argue that the context[3] and primary uses of that offering in the Law make a case for purification. I also side with the option of purification.

Even when sin was involved, the Purification Offering's blood was used to cleanse and purify the altar/sanctuary/tent of meeting and instruments. Blood was like a sanitizer or detergent. This is why the HATA'AT was sprinkled inside the tent and on the instruments. It was just like sanitizing the hospital's operation room and surgical instruments or purifying wounds so they could heal and won't spread. Likewise, the blood of the HATA'AT would act like a sanitizer or detergent, purifying the defilement caused by Israel.[4] The purification offering was not about God's wrath being poured on the poor animal or a way for God to relax his anger. It was about the blood (life) of the sacrifice being used to clean the sins (death) of Israel. Blood was even able to sanctify people.[5] Bible scholar Scott Starbuck comments:

> The two elements of purification, the cleansing of the sanctuary and the sending away of impurity, can be observed in the ritual purification of a leper by the ritual manipulation of two birds. One bird was sacrificed, and the other was set free after it and the leprous person were sprinkled with the blood of the slaughtered bird (Lev 14:2–8, 49–53).[6]

The central theme of HATA'AT is not the animal's demise (as retribution due to divine anger) but rather its blood's purifying function. One specific type of sacrificial blood can be likened to a cleansing agent. It's the kind of blood that can transform blood-stained robes into pristine white:

> They have washed their robes and made them white in the blood of the Lamb. (Revelation 7:14).

This miraculous transformation can only be understood when we liken Jesus's blood to the HATA'AT. Jesus's blood does to us what the blood of the HATA'AT did for Israel. It acts as a purifying detergent, renewing and cleaning.

As stated in Hebrews 10:10, Christ's blood washes away our sins, rendering us clean. It not only enables priests to enter God's dwelling place but also cleanses anyone who believes, allowing them entrance.

So HATA'AT perceives sin as a stain or defilement and provides a means for cleansing and purification. Although shedding of blood was involved, the concepts of wrath, anger, abuse, or torture were never part of this equation. Neither the person offering the sacrifice nor the priest ever "punished" the animal by abusing or torturing it. In fact, the one who sacrificed had to avoid cruelty at all costs. Slaughtering the animal from its neck meant a swift death with minimum pain. There are very meticulous decrees in ancient Judaism, valid in modern Judaism as well, as to how slaughtering is to be done. A great emphasis was given to killing the animal as quickly and painlessly as possible (Leviticus 1:15; 3:8; 5:8). Maimonides, a famous Middle Ages Jewish Bible commentator, explained that commandments related to slaughtering "were given to ensure an easy death for the animal." Other Jewish sages commented likewise.

All that is to say that biblical Israel brought sacrifices before God, not for God's wrath to be appeased by punishing the sacrifice. The killing was a means to an end — the animals' blood. The blood (life) had the power to purify, atone, and sanctify. It is important to remember that it is not God who needed Christ's blood; we did. Christ's blood purifies and sanctifies us, not God.

Sin

Regarding the word "sin," perhaps a better way to define sin is by considering its Hebrew term. In Hebrew, the word used for "sin" literally means "to miss."[7] If someone is shooting with a gun in a shooting range and misses the bullseye, in Hebrew, we would say that they've "sinned the target." In that respect, "to sin" is to miss the target or to fail to fulfill a goal. This linguistic association in the mind of the Hebrew speaker connects "to sin" and "to miss" together.

Thus, I would suggest that "to sin" essentially means "to miss the mark of God's will." In this context, sin arises whenever we, either as individuals or as a community, deviate from our divine potential - the image of God inherent in us. This interpretation expands the conventional understanding of sin because it isn't solely about committing egregious acts like murder or bank robbery. Sin also encompasses missed opportunities to extend goodness to others. When we fail to seize these opportunities, we are not living up to our full potential, and thereby, we 'miss the mark' of embodying God's love and grace in our actions.[8]

---

1. For example, the NAB translation translated HATA'AT in Leviticus 4:3 to "purification offering", while most other translations had "sin offering." The NIV added the following footnote to "Sin Offering":"Or purification offering; here and throughout this chapter."

2. Such as: Saadia Gaon, Samuel David Luzzatto, Jonathan Grossman, Jacob Milgrom, Yehezkel Kaufmann, and more. Samuel David Luzzatto wrote: "it's called 'Hat'at'

due to the Hituy [disinfecting] for which it's used on the corners of the alter, and since the sprinkling which is performed with the sacrifice is called 'Hituy', as is written: "Cleanse me with hyssop, and I will be clean" (Psalm 51:7), that is why the sacrifice is called 'Chata'at', not because it was intended for sin ('Chet')". (Samuel David Luzzatto's interpretation to Lev. 4:3). Jewish Bible scholar, Yehezkel Kaufmann, phrased it similarly: "if we check the sin offering (Chata'at), we will see that its main purpose was to purify from defilement or that its connected at its roots to impurity. It disinfects articles and sanctifies them (Lev. 15, 16, 18-20, 33), and not just articles that were used in the past for holy purposes, but articles that weren't used previously and could not be defiled (Ex. 29, 36-37)." Toldot Ha-Emuna HaIsraelit, part 1, p. 567.

3. Also, some would argue that as some of these hata'at-offerings would be eaten by the priests (Exodus 29:33), therefore it would make it hard to believe that the animal absorbs the sins of the people, as they would become defiled and not allowed to be eaten.

4. There is a debate whether the defilement (TOMAHA) is an actual condition, either physical or even demonic, or just a figure of speech, an idea meant to illustrate distancing from God.

5. Even before Leviticus, at mount Sinai: "Moses then took

the blood, sprinkled it on the people and said, 'This is the blood of the covenant that the Lord has made with you in accordance with all these words.'" (Exodus 24:8). The text does not say what kind of sacrifice it was. Interestingly, In Targum Onkelos (2nd century, the most important translation of the Old Testament to Aramaic), the phrase "to atone" was added to Ex. 24:8, in order to emphasize the blood was given to atone: "and Moses took the blood and threw it on the alter to atone for the people."

6. Scott R. A. Starbuck, "Sacrifice in the Old Testament," Lexham Bible Dictionary, ed. John D. Barry et al. (Bellingham, WA: Lexham Press, 2016).

7. Strong's Concordance, 2398: "chata: 'to miss'.

8. For an extended discussion on "sin," see my book: 'The "Gospel" of Divine Abuse."

COVENANT

Hebrew: BRIT

בְּרִית

In Hebrew, the term "to make a covenant" consists of two words, with the first translating to "excision" or "amputation." Rather than "making" covenants, the Hebrew context suggests physically "cutting" them—this is reflected in the English idiom "to cut a deal." The second word signifies "covenant". The idea of "cutting" a covenant denotes the incorporation of blood, which explains why biblical references to covenant-making invariably include blood.

In the current era, marked by action-packed movies, violent video games, and ceaseless news reports of violent incidents, it's hardly surprising that we often associate 'blood' with negative connotations such as violence, terrorism, warfare, suffering, and wrath. However, for the ancient Israelites, blood symbolized life, serving as a token of life itself committed to the agreement. Blood had a purifying, atoning, and healing significance. But primarily, blood symbolized LIFE, as stated in Leviticus 17:11:

> "For the life of a creature is in the blood, and I have given it to you to make atonement for yourselves on the altar; it is the blood that makes atonement for one's life."

Consider the example of Abraham. When God summoned Abraham to abandon his home and step into the unknown, He first bestowed blessings upon him—promising him heirs, land, and authority, much like the blessings in Genesis 1:28. Genesis 15 reiterates this covenant but adds a visual component that Abraham could comprehend. Abraham was instructed to gather and slaughter a heifer, a ram, a goat, a dove, and a pigeon, then split the animals in half and lay the pieces in two lines, creating a clear pathway through the center. This act was a familiar sign in the ancient Near East, symbolizing the formation of a covenant—the participants would walk the path between the slain animals, essentially declaring, "I stake my life on this." It was the most solemn form of commitment.

Interestingly, this covenant in Genesis 15 stands out because God, appearing to Abraham once he fell asleep, traversed the path between the dissected animals alone. It was a unilateral covenant with all obligations on God and none on Abraham. God was essentially pledging His life to fulfill the promises He made to Abraham—an incredibly reassuring gesture, considering God's eternal nature and inability to break an oath or die.

One might wonder why a King would enter a covenant with a peasant. When God forms a covenant with us, it's not out of necessity or want. Unlike other deities who formed deals out of self-interest, Yahweh doesn't need us and can create countless more like us. His covenant signifies His decision to care for us, even though we have nothing to offer in return. By establishing a covenant, God assures us of His unwavering love and commitment, regardless of our actions. Abraham's role was simply to believe.

This covenant also foreshadowed the one to be established through Jesus. As in Abraham's case, we were the ones who killed the sacrifice, and God was the one who made the promise.

All we have to do is believe. But the New Covenant, sealed with Christ's eternal blood, offers an everlasting guarantee of our eternal salvation—a promise far superior to any previous covenants. Like Abraham, all we need to do is trust that God will fulfill His promise of salvation to those who choose to believe (John 3:16). This unwavering assurance can provide immense confidence regarding our eternal future. I may falter and lack trust in myself with trivial matters, let alone my eternal destiny. But with God, I can rely on Him, and my soul finds peace knowing it's not up to me, a flawed being, to secure my own eternal fate.

SERPENT or SHINING ONE

Hebrew: NAHASH

Genesis 3 introduces the enigmatic figure of the serpent (Also known by other names, such as "the great dragon;" Revelation 12:9; 20:2), known as Nahash in Hebrew, which has raised questions about whether the Bible claims that a literal talking snake existed. Depictions of a serpent speaking to Eve, such as Frans Wouters' "The Temptation of Eve," are familiar sights in museums and have led many to believe that Eve was speaking with a reptile, but perhaps there was something more to it than just a talking snake.

The Hebrew root of the word "NAHASH," which refers to a serpent, is also the root of the Hebrew word for "copper," "brass," or "bronze." Although they have distinct meanings, the connection between these words becomes apparent when considering the symbolic representation of serpents in the ancient world.

Serpents were often associated with divinity, wisdom, and the idea of enlightenment, shining or gleaming. In Hebrew, the word "NAHASH" can also be interpreted as "the shining one" or "the one who shines," which is where the connection with the term "Nehoshet" (bronze/copper/brass) emerges. The International Standard Version (ISV) of the Bible, for example, translates "NAHASH" as "shining one" instead of "serpent," which highlights the shared connotation of both terms:

> "Now the Shining One was more clever than any animal of the field that the Lord God had made." (Genesis 3:1)

In this case, NAHASH is not a reptile but an impressive, shiny angelic being, much like Paul's description of Satan:

> "for Satan himself masquerades as an angel of light." (2 Corinthians 11:14)

Thus, the Hebrew word "NAHASH" can have multiple meanings: it can refer to a snake and to an impressive angelic shining being (who, perhaps, has some snake-like features). Furthermore, its consonants can form the root of a word for deception, meaning the serpent can also be understood as a deceiver or diviner. In fact, even in modern Hebrew, we will still use the word "NAHASH" to describe someone who is deceitful.

Interestingly, Eve was not alarmed when conversing with the "NAHASH," probably because she was aware of other angelic beings. However, she could not have known about the Shining One's malicious intent until it was too late, leading to the fall of both him and humanity. We better imagine Satan not as a reptile but as an impressive-looking angelic being, perhaps with some snake-like characteristics. It is plausible that the "NAHASH" became the legless reptile only after it was cursed by God.

These characteristics are also found in other divine beings throughout the Bible. For example, serpentine descriptions of divine beings appear in Isaiah 6, where God is surrounded by winged Seraphim. The term "Seraph" means "to burn" and is often associated with fire, but it is also a word for snake. Ancient Egyptian iconography and language offer further insight, suggesting that the talking serpent in Genesis 3 may be a divine, serpentine-looking being in rebellion, similar to the fiery Seraphim that worship God before His throne. In the past, serpents were frequently associated with divinity and wisdom (Matthew 10:16).

In Genesis 3:1, the serpent is described as *"more crafty than any other beast of the field that the LORD God had made."* This verse can be interpreted in two ways. Either the serpent was the craftiest beast of all, or it was much more crafty than the beasts because it was an angelic being. In the ancient Near East, there was no clear distinction between the natural and supernatural realms as we understand them today, particularly not in the Garden of Eden, where even God himself physically walked in the garden with Adam and Eve. All creatures, including humans and angels, were seen as beings created by God and possibly lived together in the same place.

The curse placed upon the NAHASH in Genesis 3 bears similarities to Egyptian Pyramid Texts, which describe serpents from the underworld attempting to obstruct the Pharaoh's journey through the afterlife. These texts also contain phrases that echo the curse on the serpent in Genesis 3, such as crawling on its belly, which may symbolize being cast down in a humiliating position before all creation.

It seems plausible that the rebellious being in Genesis 3 was a divine being with serpentine traits, capable of speech and possessing divine knowledge. The author of Genesis 3 cleverly draws parallels between their noble nature and actual snakes through the use of metaphor. The passages in Isaiah 14 and Ezekiel 28, which depict the rebellion and judgment of earthly kings, can be seen as allegorical references to the first rebellion in Eden. These passages, together with Isaiah 6 and Genesis 3, take place in a divine council setting.

It is reasonable to connect all these elements and propose that Satan was initially an impressive divine and shiny angelic being and member among other divine beings, some of which, just like him, were serpentine-looking but not (yet) actual snakes.

Not all snakes are bad

In Numbers 21, when the Israelites were walking through the Negev desert, an area known for its venomous snakes, something terrible happened. The nation of Israel, grumbling and complaining too loudly, disturbed the rest of some local poisonous snakes who started biting them, killing many. Then, Moses was sent by Israel to negotiate with God, who ordered Moses to make a bronze snake and put it up on a pole. Bronze shines brightly. Anyone who got bitten had to look at the bronze snake and would be saved from dying. For them to look up at the shiny bronze snake meant one thing - they had to accept in faith; believe what was offered. They weren't asked to do something, just to believe what God said and be saved. I assume some of the Israelites found this to be ridiculous, rejecting the offer and dying in their sin. Regardless, it was their free choice whether to believe (and be saved) or not. Now, in the New Testament, Jesus is saying:

> "Just as Moses lifted up the snake in the wilderness, so the Son of Man must be lifted up, that everyone who believes may have eternal life in him." (John 3:14)

So, we as well have to believe. But what do we see when we look up at the pole and cross? We see human sins: we see complaining, we see distrust, we see betrayal, we see false judgment, we see hypocrisy, we see desertion, we see crime, we see lies, we see manipulation, we see abuse of power, we see mockery, we see emotional torment, and we see physical torture. But ultimately, we see death. The cross is the ultimate expression of our reality. It portrays what humanity became like. It shows us how dark our hearts can get. This is perhaps why we see images of Christ hung dead on a cross in traditional churches. It is a reminder of what we are capable of and of what we did – killing our own God. And yet, we can't stop there, we need to look deeper, look harder, look further - because there is another side to the cross.

While we took Life and hung it on a tree, God turned it into a tree that gives life. We now - at least in some sense - have access once again to the tree of life: Jesus. Just as with the Israelites who did look at the snake and were saved, whoever looks at the cross, acknowledges it, believes in it - will see life, will see the resurrection, and will experience it themselves. Yes, the cross shows us how dark the reality of the human soul is, but we look at it because it shines bright; we are drawn to the light.

So now we look at the cross, and we see the source of light and life. Ultimately then, the cross is about God's love for us.

HELPER

Hebrew: EZER

No story is more famous than the Garden of Eden. Many Christians regard the Garden of Eden as a story about sin, division, and the fall. These aspects do exist, yet they are secondary. The Garden of Eden, in my interpretation, beautifully unfolds as a poignant love story. It portrays God not as an aloof entity but as a loving father tenderly caring for his cherished children. He wants the best for them, even as they fall and sin against him. Likewise, the whole Bible is the most extraordinary novel ever written, one long love story featuring a God who courts and sustains a relationship with our forefathers and foremothers. These were people who, just like you and me, were soaked in sin up to their necks. However, it's intriguing how perspectives can differ. While I (as well as most Jews) perceive a narrative brimming with love and parental concern, others interpret the Genesis account as showcasing a God who appears annoyed and furious.

The perspective one adopts when approaching the Bible has a profound impact on the understanding and interpretation of the text. A prime example of this can be found in Genesis 2:18:

> *The LORD God said, "It is not good for the man to be alone. I will make a* ***EZER*** *(helper) suitable for him."*

This verse offers two distinct interpretations. A fundamentalist perspective suggests that women were created in order to be servants:

> *The woman was created to **serve** man...The scriptures state that God created woman to **serve** man.*[1]

However, an alternative interpretation is worth considering. Notably, God refers to the woman as a "helper" instead of a "servant." This distinction prompts an important question: which party typically requires help, the weaker or the stronger? It is natural for the weaker party to seek assistance. And who should the weaker party look to for help? Not someone even less capable, but rather someone with greater strength or ability. This highlights the significance of the term "helper."

In the Old Testament, "EZER" is used to describe God as a helper to Israel, implying a role of strength and support, not subordination. Psalm 70:5 states:

> "But as for me, I am poor and needy; come quickly to me, O God. You are my **help** and my deliverer; Lord, do not delay."

The word "help" in this verse is "EZER" in Hebrew, which is the same as in Genesis. Clearly, God helping Israel does not imply that God is subordinate or inferior to human beings.

It is essential to recognize that physical strength should not be viewed as the sole determining factor in this context. While men may generally possess greater physical strength than women, women can excel in other areas, especially in emotional quality abilities, creating a balanced and complementary dynamic. This is particularly evident in many marriages, where men often seek guidance from their wives when facing challenges.

This complementary aspect of the male-female dynamic is further emphasized when examining various cultures and historical contexts. Throughout history, societies have assigned different roles to men and women based on their strengths and weaknesses. In some cultures, women have held positions of power, while in others, they have taken on more supportive roles. Despite these variations, the underlying principle of complementarity between the sexes remains constant.

The role of a servant is to obey and follow orders, while a helper's role is to provide what is lacking. Help is sought when one lacks the necessary skills or knowledge to complete a task independently, which is why we rely on experts such as mechanics, lawyers, and physicians. This concept of a helper extends beyond the realm of professional expertise, as it also applies to emotional, mental, and spiritual support. In the context of marriage, this type of support is invaluable, as it allows both partners to grow and flourish in their respective roles.

Furthermore, biblical submission addresses structure and order rather than wisdom, value, or worth. While it is true that most groups and structures have a single leader, Jesus demonstrated that true leadership entails serving one's followers (John 13). That's what EZER is all about. This notion of servant leadership is crucial to understanding the dynamics within a marriage or any relationship. A leader who serves their followers is more likely to inspire loyalty, respect, obedience and trust from those they lead. Likewise, we are not obedient to God because we are scared of Him but because He proved to be an EZER to us by being willing to give up His life for us:

> "Greater love has no one than this: to lay down one's life for one's friends." (John 15:13)

In addition to servant leadership, mutual submission is a vital component of a healthy relationship. Ephesians 5:21 states, "Submit to one another out of reverence for Christ." This verse emphasizes the importance of reciprocity and mutual respect in relationships. It is not just about one partner submitting to the other, but both partners submitting to each other out of love and respect. This establishes a model for relationships that are based on equality, respect, and partnership without demolishing the need for a leader. In this context, the role of a helper becomes even more significant, as it highlights the importance of collaboration and cooperation between partners who help and serve one another out of mutual love and respect.

Just as Eve was a crucial counterpart to Adam, filling the spaces he couldn't, so too does God operate as our "EZER" in times of need. This word reminds us that true help doesn't belittle or subordinate; it elevates and completes. Let us remember to seek God, our ultimate "EZER," in our moments of need, and to value the unique strengths and perspectives of those who complement our lives.

"You are my help and my deliverer; you are my God, do not delay." (Psalm 40:17)

---

1. Ivory Simion, "The War Between Men and Women", Xlibris, 2009. Pg 20. Bold emphasize by me.

HOLY

Hebrew: KADOSH

You may have encountered the peculiar notion that God is too holy to gaze upon or be in the presence of sinners. For instance, Philip Ryken, a council member of The Gospel Coalition, provides an explanation:

> *God the Father could not bear to look at the sin or at His Son. He had to avert his gaze. He had to shield his eyes.*[1]

The term "holy" often carries connotations of purity and righteousness in modern parlance. When someone is referred to as "holy" today, the immediate inference is that they are devoid of sin. However, the ancient Hebrew perspective offers a nuanced understanding. In biblical Hebrew, "KADOSH" translates to "holy," meaning "to be set apart" or distinct from the rest. It signifies something or someone who stands out due to a unique characteristic or purpose. While God is undeniably without sin, the term KADOSH isn't merely an assertion of His sinlessness. It's an emphasis on His unparalleled nature and distinctive essence. For instance, when God declared the seventh day as holy, it wasn't an indictment on the other six days or suggesting they were flawed. Instead, it was an affirmation of the seventh day's distinct purpose and significance. Thus, understanding holiness in its original context helps us appreciate the richness of its meaning, transcending mere opposites of good and bad. For example, in the Pentateuch, God is set apart from all other gods because He is the Creator while they are not.

Peter Gentry examined the usage of the word "holy" in the Hebrew Scriptures and concluded that:

> *The basic meaning of the word is 'consecrated' or 'devoted.' In the Scripture, it operates within the context of covenant relationships and expresses commitment.*[2]

Our God is also different in his ways. Other gods are motivated by fear and hate; Our God is love. Other gods seek revenge; Our God desires to forgive. If God's holiness meant he "could not bear to look at sin," and we all sin, then it follows that God cannot be in the presence of sinners. But this view is clearly contradicted by the different manifestations of God throughout the scriptures, the promises of the scriptures, and the very manifestation of the Son of God who came to live amidst sinners. Further, if God is omnipresent, he is always present in the fallen world. The universe continues to exist; it is preserved by the Creator's presence. Finally, there is the famous story of Job, where Satan comes before God and negotiates with him. God did not need to "avert his gaze" or "shield his eyes."

Since God is KADOSH (unique and distinct), the space He inhabits must also be holy. Consequently, when Israel contaminated the camp, it became unclean and lost its holy status. This concept mirrors the standards of an operating room in hospitals. If it becomes tainted, it ceases to be KADOSH, set apart from other rooms, and surgeries cannot be performed until it's purified. Similarly, Israel's holy place had to be purified and sanctified using the Bible's prescribed antiseptics — the blood of offerings. While Christ was indeed holy, Jesus never shunned sinners because of His holiness. Instead, He embraced them, touching, loving, and caring for them. The essence of God's holiness never acted as a barrier to His engagement with sinners. Rather, they were the primary reason for His earthly mission. Jesus epitomized holiness not just by being sinless, but by loving unconditionally, even embracing those society deemed unworthy.

Can God look at sinners?

As a sinful human, I can do nothing to earn my salvation through my own efforts. Therefore, salvation is a gift freely offered through faith in Christ. That, however, doesn't mean God hates me because I'm not perfect like he is. The teaching that sinners cannot experience God, that God hates them, or that he cannot even look at people merely because they are not perfect is unbiblical and well contradicted by both the Old and New Testaments.

In fact, the Hebrew Scriptures prove the exact opposite: a holy God who maintains relationships with the worst of sinners.

Noah, Abraham, Moses, and David were all people of faith, yet also great sinners with a very intimate relationship with God. They had a relationship with God thanks to their faith, not because they were perfect. But it doesn't stop with individuals. God loves sinners so much that he decided to even dwell among a nation of sinners. When Jews read their Bible, they see that while Israel constantly sinned, God continuously had his dwelling place amidst them in their impurity:

> *The tent of meeting, which is among them in the midst of their uncleanness. (Leviticus 16:16).*

Clearly, God does not shy away from sinners and can, in fact, look upon and dwell near them. God loves his imperfect children and seeks to draw near them and live among them.

The central message of the prophets and the New Testament is that God came down to Earth, manifested in the flesh, to pursue sinners and love them. In Jesus, God spent most of his time on earth with sinners and blessed them (Matt 9:10-17, Mark 2:15-22, Luke 5:29-39). Does this sound like a God who is so angry he's unwilling to connect or even look at sinners? On the contrary, God comes near sinners and loves them precisely because they are not perfect! No child is perfect, which is why they need parents to guide, teach, and help them grow and mature. This included the children of Israel (Deuteronomy 14:1) and any other child who ever existed:

> *For in him we live and move and have our being. As some of your own poets have said, "We are his offspring." (Acts 17:28)*

In Jesus, God even "became sin for us" (2 Corinthians 5:21), and His Spirit dwells in us, people who, although justified, still often sin.

How different is this message from the one often evangelized to Jews?

In contrast to an angry, legalistic God who hates sinners and wants nothing but to punch us all in the face and into damnation, Jesus spoke of God as loving, caring, forgiving, full of compassion, and protective Father (Matthew 23:37). A Father who's not only able to look at sinful children but makes an effort to reach out to them, to deliver and save them from their own mistakes. This is what being KADOSH is all about!

---

1. Philip Graham Ryken, "The Heart of the Cross". Crossway, a publishing ministry of Good News Publishers, Wheaton, 2005. Pg 87.

2. Peter J. Gentry, "The Meaning of 'Holy' in the Old Testament," Bibliotheca Sacra 170 (2013): 417.

WORSHIP

Hebrew: SHACHAH

In biblical times, the terms “worship” and "prayer" had a broader meaning than they do today. Most types of prayer and worship were not solely about communicating words to God; they also involved actions. However, our modern understanding of the words "worship" and "pray" has evolved to mean "talking and singing to God." For Israel, worship of God always involved sacrificing something, which taught the people of Israel important lessons. For example, to help one another, and if you want something, to be prepared to give in return.

In English translations of the Bible, several distinct Hebrew words have been translated into "worship," with the specific term varying depending on the version of the Bible. This can be seen in a variety of verses, including Job 1:20, Genesis 22:5, Exodus 33:10, Deuteronomy 26:10, Isaiah 46:6, Psalm 29:2, and many others.

The Hebrew word SHACHAH simply means "to bow." In other words, showing respect, telling others they are important and that you honor them. In ancient times, when people from various nations approached their gods to worship and pray, they would always bring a gift with them. A sacrifice. This offering could be in the form of animal or agricultural produce. They never came empty-handed, believing that by giving something to the divine, they could invite blessings and favor in return. These prayers and offerings were often made before important events such as harvests, births, or weddings as a way to seek divine protection and blessings. The underlying principle was that if you wanted to ask something of your gods, you needed to give something in return. The God of Israel was no different in this respect. Do you wish to meet and ask of Him something? Great! But lunch is on you, so don't forget to prepare and bring a nice "meal" with you when you come to the altar.

Throughout the Old Testament, we often see God rejecting Israel's attempts to worship Him and their offerings (Jeremiah 6:20; Isaiah 1:11–15; Amos 5:21–23). However, even before the formation of Israel, in the story of Cain and Abel, we understand that one cannot merely offer something to God; it must also be of high quality. Offering leftovers is not the same as offering the best you have.

The story of Cain and Abel is where we actually first meet sacrifices in the Bible.[1] These brothers did not yet have any "Law" they were following. Like many others in the Ancient Near East, they offered sacrifices to "stay on the good side" of God. You have probably heard various traditions about why God accepted Abel's offering but not Cain's. The most prominent tradition is that Abel's offering was accepted because it involved the death of an animal, while Cain's was rejected because no blood was shed. Here is an example from John MacArthur:

> *We see that Abel did what God required...H e brought the right sacrifice that was required by God...It was better because it was blood, and it was better because it was required as a sacrifice for sin.*[2]

The first problem with MacArthur's interpretation is the anachronism fallacy.[3] God did not require blood as a sacrifice for sin until much later, in the time of Moses. Moreover, the text offers no textual support for MacArthur's view. This sacrifice was not about blood and had nothing to do with forgiving sins, both ideas were foreign to Cain and Abel. The second problem is that later in Leviticus chapter two, we see that God does, in fact, accept bloodless agricultural offerings with no issues. If the children of Israel were allowed to offer agricultural produce, why would God be so upset when Cain did so? The third problem is that the New Testament's mention of the infamous story never suggested that bloodless sacrifice was the reason for God's rejection of Cain's offering.[4]

According to the text, the difference is that while Cain "brought some fruit," Abel, on the other hand, brought his very best, "fat portions from some of the firstborns." Fat firstborns? This is the "grade five Wagyu beef" of ancient times. The difference the text points out to the reader is not in the type of offering (blood vs. bloodless) but in the quality of it ("fat" and "firstborn" vs. just "some"). The quality of the sacrifice is also something God will later emphasize in the Law to Israel.[5] So, in contrast with Cain, Abel brought his very best. At the same time, Cain probably saw some bananas starting to blacken and decided they shouldn't go to waste.

Notice verse two: "Abel kept flocks, and Cain worked the soil." Cain brought fruit because he was a farmer. It is no sin to be a farmer. But as a farmer, he, too, could have picked the better portion of his fruits. But he didn't. Therefore, God's issue was not with blood but with the quality of the offering he was gifted with.

Modern Worship

The New Testament brought about a significant change, teaching a new group of Jewish believers in Jesus that when worshiping God, they no longer needed to bring the sacrifice to God. Instead, He desired for them to bring the sacrifice to the poor and needy, the sick and broken, the widows and orphans, the imprisoned, and the sinners. In this way, they worshiped Him (Matthew 25:34-40).

But then, with the destruction of the Second Temple, Jews who did not believe in Jesus could no longer offer sacrifices. The Jewish Pharisees, who opposed the corrupt priesthood, seized this opportunity to finally take over by reshaping Israel's religious practices. They introduced a revolutionary "new" idea, teaching the children of Israel that since they could not bring a sacrifice to God because the temple was gone, they could now bring it to the Pharisees in the form of coins of gold and simply repeat a couple of prayers out loud.[6]

As a result, Christians observed Jews worshiping with words alone, mistakenly thinking that no actions were ever involved (coins of gold do not "moo" or "baa" loudly on the streets). Gradually, Christianity also began to adopt this comfortable idea that worship is about words and is entirely disconnected from actions. This is why, in modern times, we associate "revival" and "worship" with music and songs. But a "worship night" should not just be about Christians going to an amplified concert with cool spotlights, whereby the crowd joins in singing words of praise. Instead, a worship night should be an evening whereby Christians go out to the streets to feed the hungry and cover the poor with a blanket. Perhaps a better name for an evening of Christian songs should be "praise night."

There is an error in modern-day Christianity- thinking that in Christ, believers are exempt from making sacrifices. We don't; we just redirect the sacrifices to offer them to society's outcasts instead. When we pray before a meal, giving thanks to God, we should also ask ourselves if there is someone, perhaps even in our own neighborhood, who could benefit from more than just our prayers. Instead of only praying for the poor and hungry, we can also feed them.

In summary, worshiping God should be done with your best and with the utmost generosity. For instance, did you notice a poor woman sitting outside McDonald's with her child when you entered to celebrate with your son? Don't merely save your doggy bag for her; buy her a meal. This is one way to truly worship God!

---

1. No, I don't believe Genesis 3:21 has anything to do with offering. I explain this at length in my book, 'The "Gospel" of Divine Abuse,' Part I, Chapter 3.

2. John MacArthur, "Abel: A Primitive Faith ," Oct 25, 2009.

3. An anachronism is a chronological inconsistency of misplacing people, events, objects, language terms, and customs in the wrong periods. The common types of anachronism in theology are verbal expressions or philosophical ideas placed outside their proper temporal domain/time.

4. Matthew 23:35; Hebrews 12:24

5. Leviticus 1:3; 2:1; 3:1; 22:21-22.

6. For farther explanation see my book "The New Kings of Israel: A Theological Survey and Critique of Rabbinic Judaism."

HATE

Hebrew: SANE

We all do wrong, and Psalm 5:5 says about God: "*You hate all who do wrong!*" So, does this mean God hates us all?

Unfortunately, today some modern fundamentalist preachers use the word "hate" in the Hebrew Bible to teach that God hates mankind. For example, perhaps the most influential reformed theologian of our time, R.C. Sproul, wrote:

> *We always say the Cliché, "God Hates the sin, but he loves the sinner." That's nonsense! The Bible speaks of Him abhorring us, and that we're loathsome in His sight, and He can't stand to even look a t us!*[1]

Likewise, on his YouTube sermon, "God Hates the Sin and the Sinner," popular reformed pastor Tim Conway[2] explains his views of the gospel like this:

> *All of mankind are children of wrath. We are objects of the hatred of God by nature. We don't deserve His love... God is not unjust to hate mankind. Because mankind is a hateful thing by nature. It ought to be hated.*[3]

Similarly, Wyatt Graham, a director of The Gospel Coalition,[4] defines the gospel in this way:

> *Jesus bore divine wrath at the cross for our sake and so protected us from it. This act implies that God hates humans since he would have poured wrath upon humans if not for the work of Christ's cross.*[5]

Marco from Reading, Pennsylvania, wrote to ask reformed Baptist pastor John Piper. The question was answered by Piper in the "Ask Pastor John" podcast: "Pastor John, what do you make of the saying, 'God loves the sinner, but hates the sin?'." John Piper's answered:

> *It is just not true to give the impression that God doesn't hate sinners by saying, 'he loves the sinner and hates the sin.' He does hate sinners.*[6]

Piper then went on quoting Psalm 5:5-6 to biblically back up his claim.

Likewise, pastor Mark Driscoll preached to his congregation the same motif:

> *The Bible speaks of God not just hating sin but sinners... Psalm 5:5, "You," speaking of God, "hate all evildoers." God doesn't just hate what you do. He hates who you are!*[7]

And David Platt wrote:

> *Does God hate sinners? Listen closely to Psalm 5:5-6: "The arrogant cannot stand in your presence;* ***You hate all who do wrong****. You destroy those who tell lies; bloodthirsty and deceitful men the Lord abhors."*[8]

The logic of these fundamentalist preachers in quoting Psalm 5:5-6 goes something like this:

1. Those who sin are sinners.

2. Everyone sins.

3. God hates sin.

4. Therefore, God hates everyone.

Practically speaking, fundamentalist preachers believe that every cute newborn, every sweet toddler, and every child playing in your neighborhood's park - God hates them.

On the surface, Psalm 5 contradicts verses like John 3:16, which state that "God so loved the world." (John 3:16). In "world," John is speaking about the people in the world, not the waters and soil. So, what John is saying is, "God so loved the sinners." But in Psalm 5, God seems to hate sinners. How do we reconcile the two?

The terms "love" and "hate" bear significant emotional weight in contemporary English language. "Hate" frequently conjures up imagery of violence, death, and fury, while "love" is often used to express intense positive emotions. People commonly use these words to describe highly charged relationships. However, the understanding and interpretation of "hate" in Biblical Hebrew diverge from these modern usages.

Psalm 5

When interpreting Hebrew Bible scriptures, we must take into account a few things. First, unless you are an Israeli, you most likely read a translation in a language other than Hebrew, the language of the Hebrew Bible. Biblical Hebrew has only so many words, so most Hebrew words have multiple meanings. Also, words change their meaning over time.[9]

Second, it is always essential to understand the broader cont ext.[10] Hebraist scholar, Mitchell Dahood, explains that Psalm 5 is about the "repudiation of false gods when one was accused of idolatry."[11] Similarly, VanGemeren, Professor Emeritus of Old Testament and Semitic Languages, says Psalm 5 is about God distinguishing himself from other gods:

> *Whereas other religions brought together good and evil at the level of the gods, God had revealed that evil exists apart from him.*[12]

So, with this context in mind, more accurate than "God hates us all" will be to say that God hates idol worshippers.

Remember, the pagans around ancient Israel would not only steal office pens and lie about how nice your dress looks today.

They would burn their babies in the fire as a sacrifice for their idols. The pagans were cruel and evil. So, it is they, in this context, that God hates. But this isn't even the main problem with how some fundamentalists use Psalm 5:5-6.

"SANE" = Avoid, Reject, Deny, Ignore

The Hebrew Bible mostly uses 'SANE' (hate) as a synonym for 'reject' or 'avoid.' According to the Ancient Hebrew Lexicon of the Bible:

> *The pictograph is a picture of a thorn, then is a picture of seed. Combined, these mean "thorn seed." The thorn, (the seed of a plant with small sharp points) causes one to turn in directions to* ***avoid*** *them.*[13]

In Romans 9:10-13, Paul clearly speaks of "hate" in a matter of election. God chose Jacob yet rejected ("hated") Esau. So biblically speaking, to hate someone is to reject or avoid them. To deny your intimacy and blessings from them. If a woman hates her husband, she pushes him away, avoids him, and leaves him. On the other hand, if she still cares for him — loves him — she will argue loudly and get upset with him. You go to battle over the things you cherish most.

Anger doesn't equal hate; apathy and distancing do. We get angry when we care. When we hate, we turn indifferent and let go.

This is why Paul says, "No one ever hated their own body, but they feed and care for their body." (Ephesians 5:29). We all know people who hate (emotionally) their body or parts of it. I hated mine when I was a fat kid with zits on my face. But as we just established, biblical hate is not about emotions or feelings of detestation. Paul was saying that no one is **avoiding/rejecting** their body. We indeed eat when we are hungry and don't avoid going to the toilet when our body asks us to — even if we emotionally "hate" how we look or something about our body.

Similarly, we should read "Esau I have SANE." It's not that God wished for him a violent and painful death (in fact, he lived a long life), but God avoided/disregarded Esau, choosing Jacob instead.

Likewise, we should read Psalm 5:5-6. God avoid-reject the idols and those who worship them – these are the evildoers. The evildoers are such because they worshipped these pagan gods and performed the evil rituals involved. God rejected idols because they made Israel do things like burn their babies alive.

The bottom line is that God may "hate" by withdrawing blessings and protection from people, rejecting their appeals, or avoiding them. However, he loves even the greatest of sinners. I know it for a fact - because I am one!

The understanding that to hate means to reject, ignore, or avoid is the only way these words of Jesus would make any sense:

> *If anyone comes to me and does not* ***hate*** *father and mother, wife and children, brothers and sis-*

ters—yes, even their own life—such a person cannot be my disciple. (Luke 14:26)

Love would not demand you “hate” (in the modern sense of it) others or your family because that would no longer be love. Besides, Jesus thought we should love everyone, our enemies included. So obviously, to "hate” your parents cannot mean hate in the modern sense of despising them. Jesus wanted his disciples to choose him over their families. Not to loathe them.

As a Jew, I had to experience Luke 14:26 when my Jewish mother first found out I believed in Jesus. She demanded I stop believing in him, and I had to **reject** her demand, choosing to follow Christ instead.

To summarize, ‘SANE’ can metaphorically be described the same way darkness or cold can. Just as darkness is the absence of light and cold is the absence of warmth, so is hate. When you reject, avoid, or ignore someone, you hate them. When you don’t want to sacrifice for a person, you hate them. God avoided the pagan evildoers, but he loves sinners.

---

1. https://www.youtube.com/watch?v=aqAuvdEtbCk
2. His preaching is promoted through the “I’ll Be Honest” platform, with nearly 100 million views on the channel’s videos.

3. "God Hates the Sin and the Sinner - Tim Conway", YouTube, Sep 18, 2018.

4. The Gospel Coalition is considered the online hub of Calvinism.

5. Does God Hate People? WyattGraham.com, April 18, 2020.

6. John Piper, "God Loves the Sinner, But Hates the Sin?", July 30, 2013.

7. Mark Driscoll, "Jesus Sweats Blood", realfaith.com

8. David Platt, "What Did Jesus Really Mean When He Said Follow Me?", page 8.

9. For further explanation, see: "Rule #3: Most Words Have Multiple Meanings" in my book "Read Like a Jew: 8 Rules of Basic Bible Interpretation for the Christian."

10. For further explanation, see: "Rule #5: Context, Context, Context." In "Read Like a Jew: 8 Rules of Basic Bible Interpretation for the Christian."

11. Mitchell Dahood S.J., Psalms I: 1-50: Introduction, Translation, and Notes, vol. 16, Anchor Yale Bible (New Haven; London: Yale University Press, 2008), 31.

12. Willem A. VanGemeren, "Psalms," in The Expositor's Bible Commentary: Psalms, Proverbs, Ecclesiastes, Song of Songs, ed. Frank E. Gaebelein, vol. 5 (Grand Rapids, MI: Zondervan Publishing House, 1991), 88.

13. Jeff A. Benner, The Ancient Hebrew Lexicon of the Bible, Virtual bookworm, 2005.

FEAR

Hebrew: YIR'AH

During my inaugural climb up the Eiffel Tower, my voyage into the vast expanse of the open ocean, and my initial experience in the heart of the Negev desert under a star-studded night sky, I was filled with a profound sense of awe and reverence. I was not scared, only felt overwhelming amazement. The grandeur of what unfolded before my eyes commanded respect. It was awe-inspiring, a sight that left me in stunned silence. This was YIR'AH.

Moses was overcome with YIRAH when he pleaded with God to witness His glory, a sight he couldn't fully behold without risking his life. He was unable to gaze directly at God. Similarly, the Israelites were steeped in YIRAH when Moses descended from Mount Sinai.

YIRAH, or awe, relates to experiencing something that surpasses one's abilities and comprehension. Undoubtedly, even the most courageous adventurer standing at the edge of an Olympic springboard would be hard-pressed to keep their heart from trembling.

The concept of "fearing God" may initially appear to imply being scared or afraid of God, but this isn't the case. Instead, fearing God encapsulates a sense of awe, respect, and reverence toward God's majesty. It's an acknowledgment of His sovereignty over all things, being all-powerful, etc. In the Old Testament, a Hebrew root with multiple meanings is Y-R-A, which can convey different ideas depending on the context. YARE & YIR'AH are examples of Hebrew words derived from this root, meaning reverence, respect, or awe. In Genesis 22:12, it is used to describe Abraham's respect and trust in God:

> “Do not lay a hand on the boy,” he said. “Do not do anything to him. Now I know that you **fear** God, because you have not withheld from me your son, your only son.”

In Proverbs 1:7, it is used to describe wisdom and knowledge:

> "The fear (YIRAT) of the LORD is the beginning of knowledge; but fools despise wisdom and instruction."

Here, YIR'AH represents a sense of respect and awe toward God, seeing Him as our supreme teacher. If you attend a seminary or university, you must respect its teachers. Otherwise, you probably won't learn much.

“Fear of the Lord” might not be best understood in modern times. The Hebrew words in the Hebrew scriptures that describe what we in modern language consider “fear” are EIMAH (terror) and PACHAD (scare). These are when you are afraid for your life, fearing someone will want to hurt you or kill you. But the word being used in Proverbs 1:7 and 9:10 is a different one. Here, it means “awe” or “reverence.”[1] In other words, wisdom begins with great respect for God, not with fearing he'll kill you. God, indeed, is a mighty warrior. But he's not a war hero because he can kill everyone in seconds. He's a war hero because he's the commander who sacrificed his life by jumping on the grenade to save those in his platoon. Understanding this truth and who God is, is the beginning of true knowledge.

In the New Testament

In the New Testament, when Paul delivered his sermon in the synagogue at Antioch, he addressed two distinct groups: "Men of Israel and you who fear God, listen" (Acts 13:16). It's interesting to note that the phrase "those among you who fear God" was directed towards the "God-fearers," Gentiles who demonstrated deep respect and reverence for God. The term "God-fearers" (or "those who fear God") in the Book of Acts refers to Gentiles (non-Jews) who were attracted to Judaism and its teachings but had not fully converted to Judaism. These individuals attended synagogue services, followed some of the Jewish laws, and respected the God of Israel, but they did not take on the full yoke of the Law, including circumcision. For example, Acts 13:26 mentions "God-fearers":

> "Fellow children of Abraham and you God-fearing Gentiles, it is to us that this message of salvation has been sent."

Paul doesn't refer to people who were scared of God. On the contrary, they were drawn to Him. They admired God's power, knew of His justice, and revered His goodness. Their fear was not one that repels but one that attracts and motivates obedience, encourages humility, and fosters a more profound, respectful relationship with God. This is the fear of God in the biblical sense, not scare.

---

1. The "Good News Bible" (by American Bible Society), for example, translated Proverbs 9:10 in this way: "To be wise you must first have reverence for the Lord."

VENGEANCE

Hebrew: NAQAM

The Hebrew word NAQAM, usually translated as "vengeance," carries a depth that challenges our limited understanding. In our minds, vengeance is often associated with pettiness, bitterness, or spite. Yet, when Scripture speaks of God's vengeance, it refers to divine justice balanced with mercy. When we contemplate vengeance or revenge, our minds might drift to devastating events, such as the atomic bombs dropped on Japan, causing the death of hundreds of thousands of civilians. Yet, the vengeance of God is starkly different from mankind's impassioned and brutal acts.

People judge others harshly, it often stems from anger or a desire to feel better about themselves, driven by various psychological and social factors. By highlighting others' perceived flaws, individuals elevate their self-perception and maintain a sense of superiority. Harsh judgment can also serve as a defense mechanism, helping cope with insecurities or self-doubt. Societal norms and expectations contribute to this tendency, as people seek belonging and validation by conforming to standards and scrutinizing those who deviate. However, this behavior perpetuates negativity and division instead of fostering empathy, understanding, and personal growth. Recognizing the motivations for harsh judgment is crucial for promoting self-awareness and cultivating a more compassionate and inclusive worldview.

A good judge embodies the principles of fairness, compassion, and wisdom, recognizing that their role extends beyond mere retribution. Rather than seeking to destroy the convict, they strive to restore them to society by focusing on rehabilitation and reintegration. Through a thoughtful approach to sentencing, a good judge carefully considers the unique circumstances of each case, balancing the interests of justice with opportunities for personal growth and redemption. By fostering a system that encourages convicts to learn from their mistakes and become better individuals, a good judge ultimately contributes to a safer and more compassionate society.

When we contemplate the concept of God's vengeance, we shouldn't allow our minds to drift towards sensationalized images of destruction and chaos, as depicted in Hollywood Armageddon movies with excessive bloodshed. This portrayal can create a misleading illusion that taking revenge and inflicting pain upon others is somehow an inherently god-like act. However, it is important to challenge this perception and recognize that the true essence of judgment often lies in empathy, understanding, and forgiveness. God's vengeance is an avenue for redemption. Isaiah 61:2 speaks of "the day of vengeance of our God," but in the same breath, it mentions "comfort all who mourn." It highlights that God's acts of justice, even when they seem harsh, have restoration and healing at their core.

In Romans 12:19, the Apostle Paul reminds us that God is the one responsible for exacting revenge, and therefore, we should refrain from seeking it ourselves:

> *Do not take revenge, my dear friends, but leave room for God's wrath, for it is written: 'It is mine to avenge; I will repay,' says the Lord.*

Paul teaches we should leave room for God's vengeance not because God will cause much more pain and destruction than we could but because God's judgment serves a purpose. Isaiah 1:24-26 sheds light on this matter:

> *Therefore the Lord, the Lord Almighty, the Mighty One of Israel, declares: 'Ah! I will vent my wrath on my foes and avenge myself on my enemies. I will turn my hand against you;* ***I will thoroughly purge away your dross and remove all your impurities. I will restore your leaders*** *as in days of old, your rulers as at the beginning. Afterward, you will be called the City of Righteousness, the Faithful City.'*

God's judgment, when understood through the lens of mercy, is a transformative force that combines justice with compassion. God's mercy offers hope, redemption, and forgiveness, allowing us to learn from our mistakes and grow spiritually. By viewing God's judgment as an opportunity for spiritual growth, we can better appreciate the nurturing aspect of divine judgment and strive to become more compassionate and spiritually attuned individuals. God's judgment is not about hurting you but about exposing the truth so the issue can be treated and you can be cured. The purpose of God's judgment is to correct people, not to condemn them.

When God executes vengeance and unleashes His wrath, He does not seek to crush, annihilate, or devastate but rather restores and purifies. The intention behind God's wrath and vengeance is to guide people on the right path, not to condemn them. This is why we should resist the urge to seek revenge and trust God to handle it. Human revenge is often fueled by emotional rage, whereas divine vengeance aims to restore the transgressor.

God's ultimate purpose in bringing transgressions to light is not to encourage others to exact wrathful judgment upon the guilty but rather to inspire us to contribute to their healing and wholeness through His grace. As Christians, we are called to reflect the love and mercy of our Heavenly Father. In situations where we feel wronged or hurt, it is essential to remember that God's wisdom and justice far surpass our own. By relinquishing our desire for revenge, we open ourselves to the transformative power of God's grace and allow His healing to work in our lives and the lives of those who have wronged us. If we retaliate, they will retaliate back in an endless circle of revenge. But if we don't, God can activate His justice and also work through their consciousness to help them understand where they acted wrong.

When we reflect on the plagues of Egypt, paralleled in some ways by those in Revelation, it's tempting to envision a cinematic display of vengeance akin to a Marvel Studios production. Yet, at its core, God's intent with the Egyptian plagues was to catalyze repentance. While the Passover narrative often centers on the Israelites, it's vital to remember the many Egyptians (Exodus 12:38) who moved by faith and chose to leave behind their homes and false deities to follow the God of Israel. The plagues played a pivotal role in their conversion. God's wrath was not simply punitive; it was an invitation to faith and salvation. As we ponder the great judgment and tribulation, let's perceive it less as vindication and more as an act of mercy, beckoning the last souls to believe. Even amid history's most tumultuous periods, God's offer of salvation remains.

As you journey through life, remember that God's vengeance serves a much higher purpose than human revenge – one of purification and redemption. Trust in his divine plan and embrace the transformative power of his grace to bring healing, wholeness, and hope to even the most broken people and situations. This is what loving your enemy is all about.

It's hard not to retaliate. It takes a lot of mental and emotional strength to forgive and also trust God's plan for justice. As we practice forgiveness, we enable God's grace to work within us, freeing us from the burden of resentment and bitterness. In doing so, we not only become more like Christ but also participate in the divine process of restoration and healing- of ourselves and of others.

ROD or SCEPTER

Hebrew: SHEVET

Several Christian books have been written to promote the belief that you should psychically abuse your children in the name of God. One famous example is the best-selling book "To Train Up a Child" by preacher Michael Pearl and his wife Debi (members of Bill Gothard's IBLP cult), in which they teach parents to hit their children with plastic tubes, whips, paddles, and belts to "break their will." They promote abusive tactics such as withholding food, giving cold showers, or leaving them outside to shame them for disobedience. "To Train Up a Child" has sold over one million copies and has been translated into twelve languages. That means millions of children have been affected by their teachings.

As one may guess, this couple used verses (out of context) to back up their abusive views biblically, specifically *Proverbs 13:24:*

> *Whoever spares the* ***rod*** *hates their children, but the one who loves their children is careful to discipline them. (Proverbs 13:24)*

In fact, the Pearl couple quotes Proverbs 13:24 several times in their short book. For example, on page 37, the couple quotes the proverb and explains that in modern times, the '**rod**' is "called whippings." And in page 46, the couple writes:

> *A spanking (whipping, paddling, switching, or belting) is indispensable to the removal of guilt in*

> *your child. His very conscience (nature) demands punishment.*

We have one Hebrew word in question that affects the understanding of this verse: SHEVET. In Pearls' interpretation, SHEVET (rod) is something you use to hit others physically. This, however, is a wrong interpretation.

Genesis 49:10 reads:

> "The SHEVET (scepter/rod) will not depart from Judah, nor the ruler's staff from between his feet, until he comes to whom it belongs and the obedience of the nations is his."

A SHEVET is a staff or rod held by both shepherds and ruling monarchs, symbolizing royal or imperial insignia and signifying sovereign authority. For a shepherd, it represents authority over sheep, while for a king, it symbolizes authority over his people.

This verse is from Jacob's blessings to his sons shortly before his death. In this specific blessing to Judah, Jacob foretells that Judah's descendants will hold royal authority. The "SHEVET" symbolizes this rule and leadership. The prophecy implies that a significant leader, usually interpreted by Christians as a reference to Jesus Christ and by Jews as referring to the Messiah, will come from the tribe of Judah and will have a lasting and significant rule. In essence, this verse emphasizes the future importance and leadership role of the tribe of Judah in Israelite history.

Proverbs 13:24

Israel was a shepherd culture. Even today, driving through the roads of modern and high-tech Israel, you will often see shepherds with their flocks. Understanding this cultural aspect will give us a better context to understand Proverbs 13:24. A shepherd carries a SHEVET (rod) to fight predators and to lead his sheep. Sheep, known as not being the wisest, will sometimes wander off at the slightest provocation. The shepherd uses the rod to block their way if they wander, leading his flock by directing the sheep back to the desired track. In this way, he disciplines them not to wander away.

The Shepherd, however, does not beat up the sheep with his rod and does not cause them distress. If panicked, they will only run away and freak out the rest. Sheep are to be disciplined with extra tenderness and gentleness, not by hurting them with whips, belts, plastic tubes, a switch, or rods.

King David, a shepherd himself, wrote:

> "Even though I walk through the darkest valley,
> I will fear no evil, for you are with me; **your rod and your staff, they comfort me**" (Psalm 23:4).

A rod will only bring you comfort if it protects you against evil, not if it breaks you.

Therefore, this proverb says the exact opposite of disciplining your child by beating them up, hosing them with water, and leaving them outside to spend the night alone. If you hate (reject/avoid) your child, you won't bother protecting, guiding, teaching, and correcting them in their life's walk. Parents are supposed to discipline their children by protecting, guiding, educating, and warning them (Proverbs 22:6). When punishment is unavoidable, there are plenty of non-traumatic ways to do it.

The way we understand our Father in heaven – to be loving, tender, and full of compassion or angry, furious, and hateful – will directly reflect in how we raise our children. Whether we like it or not, our theology shapes everything about us, including how we treat others. If people look at the cross and see the violence of a Father abusing and killing his own Son, we should not be surprised if they, too, justify their abusive behavior towards their children under the banner of "godly discipline," fearing if they won't hit them hard enough, God will.

After researching serial killers and abusers along with their family histories, I have arrived at this conclusion: One of the most effective ways to foster criminal behavior is by having hyper-legalistic parents who inflict abuse on both the body and soul of their children.

HELL

Hebrew: GÉENNA

גֵיא בֶן־הִנֹּם

When you hear the word "hell", what imagery springs to mind? Perhaps you envision an immensely dark realm (Matthew 22:13), dominated by a vast lake of searing fire (Matthew 8:12), where souls are being tortured eternally. At a glance, there's a seeming contradiction in such descriptions: how can a place be both shrouded in darkness and ablaze with fire, given that fire naturally emits light? But then again, are we even supposed to take these descriptions literally? Did Jesus not tell us that he "speaks to us parables" (Matthew 13:10-13; John 16:25)? But that's not the only challenge we are facing.

English translations frequently employ the term "Hell" as a replacement for three distinct Hebrew/Greek words: "Géenna," "Sheol," and "Hades." However, it's crucial to note that these words are not interchangeable synonyms, and each carries its unique connotations and meanings. Let's see an example.

Sheol:

> For thou wilt not leave my soul in **hell**; neither wilt thou suffer thine Holy One to see corruption. (Psalm 16:10, KJV)

Hades:

> And death and **hell** were cast into the lake of fire. This is the second death. (Revelation 20:14, KJV)

Géenna:

> And if thy right eye offend thee, pluck it out, and cast it from thee: for it is profitable for thee that one of thy members should perish, and not that thy whole body should be cast into **hell**. (Matthew 5:29)

Clearly, the English translations of these three concepts do not do justice to their original meanings.

Valley of Hinnom (Gehenna/Géenna)

The Greek word Géenna comes from the Hebrew "Gey Ben Hinom," a place outside Jerusalem.

The Valley of Hinnom (Gehenna) historically encircles Ancient Jerusalem from the west and southwest. During the late First Temple period, it served as the site of the Tophet, where some kings of Judah sacrificed their children by fire (Jeremiah 7:31). Subsequently, the prophet Jeremiah cursed this valley (Jeremiah 19:2–6). The Book of Isaiah refers to it as the "burning place" (Isaiah 30:33).

Isaiah 66:24 describes Jews who will come to restore Jerusalem witnessing "the dead bodies of the men who have rebelled against me. For their worm shall not die, their fire shall not be quenched, and they shall be an abhorrence to all flesh." This portrayal of the aftermath of God's judgment on Israel can easily be juxtaposed with Jeremiah's account of the dead cast into the Valley of the Son of Hinnom during the Babylonian siege.

Josephus, the 1st-century historian, recounts that during the Roman siege of Jerusalem, bodies were hurled over the city walls into the surrounding valleys, as there was no space left for burials within the city (Jos. War 5.12.3).

Rabbi David Kimhi, in his commentary on Psalms 27:13 from around 1200 AD, noted that in this dreaded valley, fires were perpetually maintained to consume the waste and corpses deposited there. The Talmud also links the location with fire and smoke (Erovin 19).

In Mark 9:43-48, Gehenna is depicted as a place of "unquenchable fire," "the worms that eat them do not die, and the fire is not quenched." Matthew's reference to the "Gehenna of fire" seems to be a condensed rendition of this combined imagery.

Clearly, to first-century Jews, Gehenna was a tangible location outside Jerusalem, infamous for its disgustingness, repulsiveness and revulsion. It was emblematic of fire, refuse, and death.

To be thrown into Géenna

Let's examine Matthew 5:27-29 as a case study: What did Jesus really mean when he said that men looking at a woman with lust will end up in Géenna?

First, it's hard to imagine that Jesus, who only a few verses earlier said, "Do not think that I have come to abolish Law or the Prophets" (5:17), would contradict both himself and Moses in saying something like: "Forget what the Law said! From now on, if you are about to lust, take a knife and cut your eye out, or else you will spend eternity in hell!" Clearly, Jesus was not telling people to literally dismember their bodies, or else we would all be blind. Besides, blind men can still "lust in their hearts." Obviously, Jesus, the master of parables, had to be speaking figuratively.

In his commentary[1] on Matthew, Theologian Francis Wright Beare points to the challenges in giving a literal interpretation to these words of Jesus:

> If this [Mt. 5:29-30] is to be taken as a 'demand' of Jesus, then it must be said that he is demanding the impossible, for it is the universal experience that the sexual impulses are uncontrollable.

So, what could Jesus have meant? First, remember Jesus wasn't talking to one person in particular. His audience was the Jews, the people of Israel. He was warning them of something that had to do with that place called Geena. But of what?

Géenna

When Jesus was teaching about adultery, he said that it's better to lose one body part, like your eye, than to have your entire body end up in "Gehenna" (Matthew 5:27-29). Was Jesus truly saying that if you were turned on sexually by looking at another person and fantasizing about them, even momentarily, you'd end up in hell forever? Was Jesus teaching us to literally dismember body parts, like our eyes, to ensure our salvation? If so, doesn't Jesus know that we don't need eyes to imagine and fantasize? Also, since it is the universal experience that sexual impulses in our heads are uncontrollable, why would God create us this way, to begin with, and give us impossible standards? How is that fair? Or maybe the interpretation that suggests Jesus spoke of eternal punishment is all one big misunderstanding?

Let's take a step back. We already established that the Greek word Gehenna ("hell") comes from the Hebrew GEHINNOM, meaning "the Valley of Hinnom." This was a valley outside Jerusalem used as a dump. As with all city dumps, the poor, including lepers, often scavenged through the garbage. To eliminate waste and refuse, it was burned. Fudge[2] explains:

> The term conveyed a sense of total horror and disgust...Gehenna was a place of undying worm and irresistible fire, an abhorrent place where crawling maggots and smoldering heat raced each other to consume the putrefying fare served them each day.

Therefore, in the "valley of hell," there were always flames of fire somewhere. Gehenna-hell was a real place full of disgusting waste burned in the fire, not a spiritual place across the heavens.

If you had to scavenge in Gehenna, in hell, it meant you got to the lowest point in your life—a place of great shame.

When New Testament texts using Gehenna are considered,[3] things become even more apparent. Jesus symbolically uses Géenna-hell (Valley of Hinnom) to teach about great shame. It is what people who lived or scavenged through the valley felt. Constant shame and embarrassment. This is why living with one eye is better "than to have two eyes and be thrown into the fire of Géenna" (Matthew 18:9). If you were caught committing adultery, you would become an outcast of society and find yourself living in shame in a dumpster. New Testament scholar N.T. Wright[4] explains:

> When Jesus was warning his hearers about Gehenna, he was not, as a general rule, telling them that unless they repented in this life, they would burn in the next one. As with God's kingdom, so with its opposite: it is on earth that things matter, not somewhere else.

National Rebuke

On a national level, Jesus's message was extreme: Unless you'd turn back from your wicked ways, you would find yourselves scavenging in the smoldering rubbish heap. When Jesus warned Israel, he was warning them of something very real. This is exactly what happened to Israel when Rome later destroyed Jerusalem, leaving the people of Israel to starve in shame in ruins.[5]

Imagine being a Jewish person in a legalistic society that would not tolerate any form of sexual immorality and would show no grace or forgiveness for any of it. Instead, they would take everything away from you, leaving you to scavenge for leftovers in the trash thrown into the Valley of Hinnom. In that religious society, being caught in adultery meant being ostracized and literally "thrown to hell."

This is why living with one eye is better "than to have two eyes and be thrown into the fire of hell" (Matthew 18:9). If you were caught in adultery, you would find yourself living in constant shame in the city dump; hell.

And this is also why lusting in your mind could lead to hell, because your thoughts turn to actions, and some actions, especially in an unforgiving religious society, can result in that graceless society taking everything from you, throwing you to rot in hell. Not only was your relationship severed, but you became an outcast as well.

For this reason, being able to control your thoughts is so crucial. But there is an even more important lesson here. It is not God who caused people to end up in the Valley of Hinnom; it was the people— a religious society. God, on the other hand, desires that even sinners will live with dignity, be rebuilt, and become self-sufficient.

When God witnesses people committing adultery, he does not seek to shame or abandon them. He is not interested in casting them into hell. How do I know? Because when religious people brought a woman caught in adultery before Christ, Jesus did the very opposite of what the religious leaders hoped for. He forgave her: "*Then neither do I condemn you,*" *Jesus declared.* "*Go now and leave your life of sin.*" (John 8:11). She did indeed sin. But Jesus did not condemn her. The legalists did.

Religious individuals may eagerly condemn to hell, but Jesus, rather than judging, showed grace. He understood that love is a far more powerful catalyst for the regeneration of the human heart and conscience than the punishment of hell.

Other possible interpretations are available. But whatever Jesus meant, clearly, he did not teach salvation by self-torture. Christ was also not teaching Israel about eternal destruction and separation from God just for looking at a woman with lust. Paul the apostle, the master of theology, not once used the word Géenna in reference to eternal separation from God.

---

1. F. W. Beare, The Gospel According to Matthew: Translation, Introduction, and Commentary (Hendrickson, 1987). p. 152.
2. Fudge, The Fire That Consumes, 161-162.
3. Matthew 5:22, 29, 30; 10:28; 18:8-9; 23:15, 33; Mark 9:43-47; Luke 12:5; James 3:6.
4. N.T. Wright, Surprised by Hope: Rethinking Heaven, the Resurrection, and the Mission of the Church. HarperOne, 2008. Pg. 176.
5. In year 70 AD, following a brutal five-month siege, the Romans destroyed Jerusalem and the Second Temple.

FAITH

Hebrew: EMUNAH

In the Hebrew language, the concepts of "belief," "trust," and "faith" are intricately connected through the shared root word:

- Belief = EMUNAH
- Trust = EMUN
- Faith = EMUNAH

That root is also where the word "amen" comes from. This is why when you end a prayer, you end it with "amen," "I trust." This linguistic connection highlights the deep interrelatedness of these ideas for native Hebrew speakers. We believe in Jesus, but we also trust him and have faith he will live up to his promises!

In the realm of sports, for instance, a coach might place their faith, trust, or belief in a particular football player, confident in their ability to excel as the team captain or score crucial goals. This trust extends beyond simple expectations of performance, encompassing an unshakable conviction in the player's potential and dedication to their role.

In a similar vein, during ancient Israelite times, disciples would often put their trust in a teacher-rabbi to provide guidance and mentorship. This relationship was not exclusively centered on matters of salvation or eternal life but rather on the everyday pursuit of spiritual growth and moral development. Throughout the era of the Second Temple Judaism, it was common for Jewish men to choose a teacher-rabbi to follow. This individual was someone they believed in and trusted to lead them as a life coach, taking on the responsibility of guiding them on the path to a life that honors and glorifies God. In other words, they had EMUNAH in them!

Faith can be understood as a mental assent or agreement to a particular belief or idea. For instance, believing that Elizabeth II was the Queen of the United Kingdom or that one's parents are indeed their parents requires a simple acceptance of these facts as true.

The Israelites always assumed the God of Israel would save them due to their faith, regardless of their works, which affected their daily lives. The "faith vs. works" argument in Christianity is foreign to the Jewish people. Judaism teaches and believes that "All of the Jewish people, even sinners and those who are liable to be executed with a court-imposed death penalty, have a share in the World-to-Come." (Mishnah Sanhedrin 10:1).

Works and repentance have always been crucial for Jews, as they believed these influenced God's blessings on them in this world and their rewards in the afterlife. However, they never equated works and repentance with salvation, which they considered to be by faith alone. Later, when John and Jesus called Israel to national repentance, similar to the prophets before them, it was to save Israel from "the wrath of God." In Old Testament terms, this meant God would withdraw His protection, leaving Israel exposed. In the context of Second Temple Judaism, this implied that Jerusalem and the temple would be destroyed, an event that indeed transpired in 70 AD due to Israel's rejection of Christ. Israel's failure to repent profoundly affected them—God did not shield them, synonymous with God's wrath, resulting in their significant banishment and exile from their homeland.

In relation to the Law, it was always about how to live a blessed life, which is why the Law never mentioned anything about salvation or heaven and hell. Of course, some laws had a spiritual aspect, yet the Law was Israel's constitution, not "a guide to heaven for dummies." The Old Testament was never about getting saved through works; it was always about EMUNAH:

> "Abram [had] EMUNA [in] the LORD, and he credited it to him as righteousness." (Genesis 15:6)

> "The righteous person will live by his EMUNA." (Habakkuk 2:4)

In the context of Christianity, EMUNAH represents a personal, mental response independent of one's actions, through which individuals are persuaded that eternal life is assured in Jesus Christ by virtue of His death and resurrection. To believe in Jesus is to believe His words and promises. Faith, in this sense, is passive. Just as a child believes their parents are their mother and father without any action beyond acknowledging it as true, Christians accept Jesus' teachings and promises—including the assurance of eternal life—by taking Him at His word. A child doesn't have to prove his worthiness by actions. He merely has EMUNAH in his parents. Faith is the channel through which God saves us. This is also why throughout the New Testament, Jesus consistently offered forgiveness of sins to individuals based on their simple faith:

> Some men brought to him a paralyzed man, lying on a mat. When Jesus saw their **faith**, he said to the man, "Take heart, son; your sins are forgiven." (Matthew 9:2)

This passage highlights the transformative power of faith, as a mental assent, in providing the foundation for forgiveness and the promise of eternal life. The paralyzed man didn't (and couldn't) do a thing but believe; have faith in Jesus to save him.

Belief, while a seemingly straightforward concept, can be difficult to implement in practice. In a world where disappointment and betrayal are commonplace, trusting others can be challenging. The disciples of Christ experienced this challenge firsthand as they learned to trust Jesus. Initially, their willingness to follow Him was a simple act of faith, not fully understanding who He was. Had Jesus immediately claimed to be the Son of God, they might have fled, thinking Him delusional. Instead, He gradually gained their trust - increasing their EMUNAH in Him – by performing miracles, attracting not only the disciples but also other followers, including some rabbis (Matthew 8:19).

Jesus' name in Hebrew, YESHUA, means "salvation." To have EMUNAH in Yeshua [salvation] is to trust/faith/believe He will save you!

However, the connection between believing in Jesus and the concepts of eternal life and salvation was not immediately apparent to the disciples. It wasn't until the middle of the Gospel of Matthew that Simon Peter finally recognized Jesus as "*the Messiah, the Son of the living God!*" (Matthew 16:16). Before this revelation, Simon Peter's faith and trust in Jesus were limited, viewing Him primarily as a great rabbi-teacher. Consequently, when interpreting phrases like "believed in Jesus" or "trusted Jesus," it is essential to consider the context.

For example, in Matthew 8:25, when the disciples cried out, "*Lord, save us!*" they were not referring to eternal salvation. Instead, they were seeking Jesus' help in saving them from physical danger as their boat was on the verge of sinking (verse 24). Their EMUNAH in Jesus's power, wisdom, and ability to protect them from drowning was rooted in the present moment. Do you remember what Jesus' reply was to them? *"You of little* EMUNAH, *why are you so afraid?"* Having faith in Jesus, in this case, was about trusting Him to literally and physically save.

Over time, however, the disciples also learned to trust that Jesus would provide eternal safety, even if they did not fully understand what that even meant. Their faith, though simple and child-like, was enough to experience salvation:

> For it is by grace you have been **saved**, through EMUNAH—and this is not from yourselves, it is the **gift** of God, not by works, so that no one can boast. (Ephesians 2:8)

While people can boast about their achievements, grace cannot be earned or boasted about. It is a free, unmerited gift from God, emphasizing the importance of EMUNAH and humility.

Interestingly, several centuries ago, John Calvin interpreted the phrase "It is the gift of God" to mean that faith itself was the gift. However, contemporary Greek scholarship largely contends that it is salvation, rather than faith, that constitutes the gift.[1] Faith is a choice of free will. It is up to us if we believe and in what (or who) do we believe. Love cannot be forced upon someone, or else it will no longer be love. In return for our faith (acknowledging God's love for us through Jesus Christ), God gives us the gift of salvation. This perspective emphasizes the importance of personal choice and commitment in embracing faith and, consequently, receiving the divine gift of salvation.

Faith and Psychology

You've probably heard about Abraham Harold Maslow, a psychologist best known for creating the "Maslow's Hierarchy of Needs." A theory of psychological health predicated on fulfilling innate human needs in priority, culminating in self-actualization. According to Maslow's Hierarchy of Needs, our most profound need is to feel safe and secure. I believe this need also drives us when we meditate about the afterlife and why we want to make it into Heaven. We want to be safe forever. As we all slowly die, this is what we long for the most and our greatest hope.

In accordance with Maslow's hierarchy of needs, safety and security are fundamental requirements for the emotional and mental well-being of all living creatures. This principle can (and should) also be applied to our faith. It seems fitting that God, who designed our mental and emotional needs, also addresses our deep-seated desire for eternal security. The hope of the gospel is rooted in the assurance of eternal salvation, regardless of the trials and tribulations we face. Jesus, recognizing this essential need, promised complete safety and security to those who believed in Him no matter what happened to their bodies.

Jesus promised, "*Your faith has saved you; go in peace.*" (Luke 7:50). You can only "go in peace" and have true peace in your heart if you have real confidence and assurance that you are indeed saved. Such confidence and assurance are only possible is God's salvation is free and has nothing to do with your performances.

Children trust their parents will not abandon them, even when they throw tantrums in public spaces. In the same way, our heavenly Father will not forsake us when we experience moments of weakness or doubt. Even faith as small as a mustard seed or as innocent as that of a child is sufficient for God to save.

I believe God is looking for any excuse to bring on board as many as possible because His heart is huge and has a lot of space!

The notion that one can lose their salvation fails not only to understand the concept of EMUNAH but also to fully comprehend the depth of love and compassion that characterizes our loving Father. If God intended for us to live in constant anxiety about our salvation, He would not be described in the Bible as a 'Father,' but rather as an 'Employer.' Our Father loves us, and His salvation is guaranteed even when we fail or have doubts: "*If we are not faithful, he remains faithful, because he cannot be false to himself.*" (2 Timothy 2:13)

Fearing doubt often comes from a misunderstanding of the inherently flexible nature of faith. It's okay to have doubts; God won't despise you for it. In fact, EMUNA is a living, flexible thing. If it weren't, it couldn't grow. Many faith giants in the Bible grappled with doubt, and their EMUNA grew stronger through it. Without ever experiencing doubt, our faith remains simplistic and superficial. Peter's journey exemplifies this. One day, filled with EMUNA, he proclaimed his willingness to die for Jesus (Matthew 26:35), but the very next day, he denied Jesus three times (Matthew 26:69-75). Reflect on this: Peter denied Jesus three times before the crucifixion, yet after His resurrection, he affirmed his love for Jesus three times (John 21). It was fear of retribution that led Peter to deny Jesus, but it was love that drove him to express his affection for Jesus. Throughout this period, not only did Peter not lose his salvation, but his EMUNA also deepened, albeit through challenges.

But it wasn't only Peter who lost EMUNAH. Jesus experienced abandonment by all of His closest friends, those one would expect to stand by Him unconditionally: "*Then everyone deserted him and fled.*" (Mark 14:50). However, Jesus did not harbor resentment towards them. In the aftermath of His resurrection, Jesus said:

> Go and tell my **brothers** to go to Galilee; there they will see me. (Matthew 28:9-10)

Despite their abandonment, Jesus's first priority after being resurrected was to reunite with them. Notice that Jesus referred to them as His "brothers." Not "students," not "friends," not "those idiots who abandoned me just when I needed them the most." He referred to them as "my brothers!" a term of endearment and unusual closeness still used in Israel today between close friends in particular. This is especially comforting, as it reminds us that even when we waver in our faith, Jesus remains steadfast and forgiving, never turning His back on us.

In both religious and secular contexts, people often cut ties with those who have wronged them. Jesus, however, defied this common reaction by embracing those who had betrayed Him and seeking their company. He called them "brothers," demonstrating the true depth of His love and forgiveness.

What about you? Are you willing to look at people who offended and deserted you as your brothers and sisters?

---

1. In the past, some have objected to this argument, contending that the Greek noun for "salvation" is also feminine, thus, it cannot be the antecedent of "gift." While it is true that the Greek noun, "salvation," is a feminine form, the verbal construction found here used in connection with a neuter pronoun ("this") requires that the antecedent must also be neuter, thus, "salvation" [understood], not "faith" (Lockhart, 86; Cottrell, 200).

Epilogue

THANK YOU! (TODA)

I hope you've found value in exploring these 15 Hebrew words. All these insights are adapted from my book, ***The "Gospel" of Divine Abuse***

This small book is a volume in my "micro books" series available on Amazon. If you've found this book enriching, please, I'd be deeply grateful if you could rate it and/or pen a brief review on Amazon. Your feedback would be a tremendous encouragement! And don't forget to check out my other books. If you are especially intrigued by Bible interpretation from a Hebrew perspective, see my other book: "Read Like a Jew: 8 Rules of Basic Bible Interpretation for the Christian."

P.S. TODA means 'Thanks' in Hebrew.

Made in the USA
Monee, IL
01 April 2024

56164686R00066